Low Carb S

Delici... ... Simple Low Carb Recipes For Healthy Living

Sara Banks

Symbol LLC

LOW CARB SLOW COOKER

DELICIOUSLY SIMPLE LOW CARB RECIPES FOR HEALTHY LIVING

INTRODUCTION

LOW CARB SLOW COOKER CHICKEN AND SEAFOOD

LOW CARB SLOW COOKER PORK RECIPES

LOW CARB SLOW COOKER BEEF RECIPES

LOW CARB SLOW COOKER TURKEY RECIPES

LOW CARB SLOW COOKER VEGETABLE RECIPES

CONCLUSION

FREE PREVIEW MASON JAR MEALS

Introduction

I want to thank you and congratulate you for purchasing "Low Carb Slow Cooker - Deliciously Simple Low Carb Recipes For Healthy Living"

Inside this recipe book are some fantastic and delicious low carb recipes for your slow cooker that you will just absolutely love. If you want to eat healthy and lose weight with the low carb lifestyle then this recipe book is for you. It's time to take advantage of these amazing recipes and your slow cooker.

I have even included nutritional information with each recipe to help you with your health and weight loss goals. Which one will be your favorite? .

Let's get started!

Thank-you

Sara Banks

We know carbohydrates are important since they are the fuel that our body needs to function optimally; however, we need to be careful about the kind of carbohydrates we take or else you will find yourself always gaining weight even when you don't eat as much. So, how do you determine the kinds of carbohydrates to eat? Simple carbohydrates are easily and quickly digested, they have what is known as a high glycemic index. This is a ranking on how fast a carbohydrate is converted into sugar in your body to produce energy for the body cells. Foods with high glycemic index can raise your blood sugar to very high levels than your body can manage. This can cause hormonal imbalance leading to the increased secretion of insulin, which helps regulate blood sugar level. Since insulin is also a fat storing hormone, high amounts of insulin in the body will necessitate the storage of more fat for energy. This will lead to rapid weight gain and obesity. This creates the need for everyone to check on their carbohydrate intake to avoid the health risks that may accompany a high carbohydrate diet.

Foods with high carbohydrate content are referred to as fast-carbs and should be avoided, as they can be a ticking time bomb. If you adopt a regular habit of consuming fast carbs, you will develop a high risk of developing diabetes type 2, excessive and rapid weight gain or obesity, which might lead to a lot more other health risks such as high blood pressure and cardiovascular diseases. Most processed foods fall under this category of simple carbs or fast carbs and should be given at all costs.

It is advisable to develop a low carb diet lifestyle by only consuming healthy foods with a low glycemic index, as not all foods with low glycemic index are healthy. For instance, while baked potatoes have a higher glycemic index as opposed to potato chips, baked potatoes are a far much healthier option. If you have to take carbohydrates, then embrace complex carbohydrates high in fiber and which take a long time to be digested hence not causing spikes in the blood sugar levels.

While adopting a low carb diet is exiting, most people don't have time to cook and they easily go back to their poor eating habit. Therefore, the slow cooker also known as the Crockpot is the secret weapon behind the perfect working of the low carb recipes. They make it possible to cook foods for long durations at low temperatures while maintaining their rich taste and compromise less on the quality of nutrients in the cooked foods unlike with the case of fast cooking.

We will have a look at delicious low carb slow cooker recipes that can assist you kick-start your low carb lifestyle. The foods are simple to cook and delicious to indulge in, as you will later find out as you try some of them but more importantly is the simple fact that they are very healthy.

Low Carb Slow Cooker Chicken and Seafood
Slow Cooker Poached Salmon

Servings: 4 to 6

Ingredients

2 pounds of skin –on salmon (4-6 fillets), farm-raised preferably

Coarse sea salt, Lemon wedges and olive oil for serving

Kosher salt and freshly ground black pepper

1 teaspoon of kosher salt

1 teaspoon of black peppercorns

5 sprig fresh herbs (such as tarragon. Italian parsley or dill

1 bay leaf

1 shallot thinly sliced

1 lemon thinly sliced

1 cup dry white wine

2 cups of water

Directions

Mix water, black pepper corns, herbs, bay leaf, shallots, lemon, wine and salt in a slow cooker and cook on high heat for around 30 minutes. Season top of salmon with pepper and salt then put in the slow cooker with the skin side down. Cover with a lid and cook on low heat until the salmon flakes gently with a fork and is opaque. Check on the desired doneness after about 45 minutes and cook until the desired doneness has been achieved. Sprinkle salt on the salmon and drizzle the olive oil. Serve with the lemon wedges.

Nutritional information

520 calories, 30.5g fat, 6.9g saturated fat, 1.9 g carbohydrates, 0.2 g fiber, 0.6 g sugars, 46.5 g protein, 124.7 g cholesterol, 723 mg sodium

Crockpot Seafood Stew

Servings: 6

Ingredients

2 tablespoons fresh parsley, chopped

½ teaspoon salt

1 teaspoon dried basil leaves

¼ teaspoon red pepper sauce

2 tablespoons olive oil

1 cup baby carrots, sliced

3 cups sliced quartered roma tomatoes

1 teaspoon splenda

½ cup green bell pepper, chopped

1 cup water

½ teaspoon fennel seed

½ lb peeled and deveined shrimp

1 lb cod cut into an inch slices

1 bottle (8 ounce) clam juice

2 cloves garlic, finely chopped

Directions

Mix garlic and oil in a crockpot. Add tomatoes, carrots, fennel seed, bell pepper, clam juice and water then stir.

Cover and cook for 8 to 9 hours on low heat or until the vegetables are tender. Around 20 minutes before serving, stir in the shrimp, cod, basil, splenda, pepper sauce and salt. Cover and cook on high until the fish flakes with a fork. Add in the parsley and stir.

Nutritional information per serving

Calories: 177.4, Protein: 25.2g, Total Fat: 5.8g, Total Carbs: 4.7g, Dietary Fiber: 1.1g, Sodium: 331.5g, Cholesterol: 98.9g

Crockpot Shrimp

Servings: 4

Ingredients

1 ½ cup shrimp, cooked

1 can cream of shrimp soup

2 egg yolks beaten

4 ounces mushrooms, drained and sliced

¾ cup evaporated milk

Instructions

Put all ingredients except the egg yolks in the slow cooker. Cover and cook for 4 to 5 hours on low. Add in the egg yolks and stir then cook for another hour. You can serve this with some vegetables.

Nutritional Information per serving

Calories: 194, Protein: 17g, Carbohydrates: 9 g, Fat: 9g

Slow Cooker Buffalo Chicken

Servings: 6

Ingredients

1 ½ cups of chicken broth

2 cloves of garlic

1 small onion (quartered)

2 whole stalks of celery

2 whole carrots

2 pounds of boneless, skinless chicken

Salt and pepper to taste

½ - 2/3 cup of store bought buffalo sauce

2 tablespoons of butter

Directions

To a slow cooker, add the chicken breasts, whole garlic cloves, onions, whole carrots, the celery ribs, whole garlic and chicken broth. Use the salt and pepper to season. Set your cooker on high heat and cook for 4 hours. Discard everything except the 1/3 cup of cooking liquid and the veggies. Use a fork to shred the chicken into small pieces. If you wish to use the buffalo sauce and butter, add it in then let it cook for 15 extra minutes.

Nutritional information per serving

154.4g calories 33.9g protein,1.6g fiber, 8.1 g carbohydrates, 3.5g fat,

Slow Cooker Jerk Chicken

Servings: 12

Ingredients

1 red pepper

2 tablespoons of white vinegar

1 ½ teaspoons of salt

4 habanero peppers (seeded)

4 scallions

2 teaspoons of allspice berries

1 tablespoon of minced fresh ginger

2 tablespoons of fresh thyme

4 garlic cloves

¼ cup of fresh lime juice

1 ½ pounds of bone-in and skinless chicken breasts

1 ½ pounds of boneless and skinless chicken thighs

Salt and pepper to taste

Directions

Put chicken in slow cooker then mix the rest of the ingredients together in a blender. It is best to add in the habaneros one after another, as you taste to determine the best level of heat required. Pour the blended mixture over the chicken and then cook for at least six hours in the slow cooker. Shred your chicken before serving.

Nutritional information per serving

106. 1 calories, 18.9 g of proteins, 2 g of fiber, 1.8 g of carbohydrates, 2.2 g of fat

Crockpot Thai Green Curry Chicken

Servings: 8 cups

Ingredients

1 red onion (sliced)

1 can of baby mini corn (drained)

1 bag of stir fry fresh veggies (you can opt for your own combinations)

3 tablespoons stevia

2 ½ pounds of chicken breasts (cut into small pieces)

4 garlic cloves (minced)

3 tablespoons of green curry paste

1 ½ cans of light coconut milk

2 tablespoons almond flour

Directions

Whisk together the, green curry paste, stevia, coconut milk and garlic in the bottom of a Crockpot. Add the chicken, the onion, the vegetables and the baby corn. Go ahead and cook for at least 4 hours. Whisk the almond flour and the 2 tablespoons of water then add to the Crockpot and cook for an extra 30 minutes and make sure the curry is thick enough.

Nutritional information per serving

240.9 calories, 1.5 g of fiber, 35.5 g of proteins, 5.9 grams of carbohydrates, 10.5 g of fat,

Crockpot Creamy Salsa Chicken

Servings: 8

Ingredients

1 jar salsa (16 ounce)

1 can of cream mushroom soup

6 large boneless chicken breasts (approximately 3 pounds)

Directions

Put the chicken breasts at the bottom of a slow cooker; combine salsa and soup. Pour over the chicken breasts and set the slow cooker on low heat. Cook for at least 4 hours and then take a fork and stir the chicken around so that it shreds. In case it does not shred, cook further for about 30 minutes. You can use tortilla or just use it as it is. You may opt to use onion, avocado or cheese as optional toppings.

Nutritional information per serving

254.6 calories, 40.8g of protein, 0.3 g of fiber, 5.3 g of carbohydrates, 624.9mg of sodium, 101.7mg of cholesterol, .6.6 g of fat,

Slow Cooker Chicken Stroganoff

Servings: 4

Ingredients

1 (10.75 ounce) can-condensed cream, chicken soup

1 (8 ounce) package of cream cheese

1 (7 ounce) package of dry Italian style salad dressing mixture

1/8 cup of butter

4 skinless, boneless chicken breasts halves (cubed)

Directions

Place the chicken, butter and dressing a slow cooker and mix together. Cook on low heat for 6 hours. Add in the soup and cream cheese and mix. Cook on high heat for an extra ½ hour or until it is warm and heated through.

Nutritional information per serving

456 calories, 1603g of sodium, 33.4 g of proteins, 0g of fiber, 31g fat, 136ng cholesterol, 9.5 g of carbohydrates.

Low Carb Crockpot Chicken Parmesan Soup

Yield: 4 extra large bowls

Ingredients

¼ teaspoon nutmeg

1/3 cup of grated parmesan cheese

2 chicken breasts (diced, boneless, skinless)

1 teaspoon Better Than Bouillon beef base

½ teaspoon of poultry seasoning

1/8 cup of fresh parsley (chopped)

2 diced stalks of celery

1 cup of Zucchini (diced)

1 chopped yellow onion (medium sized)

1/8 teaspoon of pepper

½ teaspoon salt

1 cup of water

4 cups of chicken broth

Directions

Put all the ingredients in a slow cooker leaving out the chicken, nutmeg and the parmesan. Cover and cook on low for about 5 hours or on high for about 3 hours. Add nutmeg and diced chicken then cook for approximately 1 more hour or until the chicken is tender then stir the parmesan cheese into soup and add in additional salt and pepper as required.

Nutritional information per serving

Approximately 3.9 g of net carbohydrates per serving

Chicken Fajita Soup

Servings: 14

Ingredients

1 ½ lbs chicken breast

14.5 oz can tomatoes, diced

32 oz chicken stock

1 diced orange bell pepper

1 diced yellow bell pepper

6 oz thinly sliced mushrooms

1 diced onion

4 tablespoons taco seasoning

4 minced garlic cloves

1 tablespoon garlic salt

2 tablespoons chopped fresh cilantro

Directions

Add all the ingredients into the crockpot, cover and cook for six hours on low. Shred the chicken breasts using two forks, then cover and cook for another one hour.

Nutritional Information per serving

Calories: 73, Protein: 12g, Carbs: 4 net grams, Fat: 1.5g

Crockpot Shredded Chicken

Servings: 10

Ingredients

5 lbs skinless and boneless chicken breast

2 chopped green bell peppers

2 chopped onions

For juice:

4 limes

½ tablespoon ground black pepper

1 tablespoon sea salt

½ cup water

Lime zest

Pinch of cayenne pepper

Directions

Put the chicken breast in the crockpot and cover with peppers and onions. For the juice mix the juice ingredients and pour this in the crockpot over the chicken.

Cook on low for around 8 hours. Towards the end of cooking, shred the chicken. Serve this with brown rice, vegetables or whole grain tortillas.

Nutritional Information per serving

Calories: 77, Protein: 8.9g, Total Carbs: 6.5g, Dietary Fiber: 1.0g, Sodium: 25.0mg, Cholesterol: 20.6mg

Low Carb Chicken Stew

Servings: 6-8

Ingredients

4 boneless and skinless chicken breasts cut into small pieces

1 teaspoon salt

1 (14-ounce) can beef stock

¼ teaspoon pepper

4 chopped celery stalks with leaves

1 onion, chopped

1 (26-ounce) can of chopped tomatoes

1 chopped carrot

3 cups chopped cabbage

Parmesan cheese

2 handfuls of baby spinach

Directions

Put all the ingredients in the crockpot except the spinach and cook for five hours on high then add the spinach, one hour to completion of cooking time. Serve with parmesan cheese on top.

Nutritional Information per serving

Approximately 8.6 grams of net carbs

Low Carb Slow Cooker Pork Recipes
Slow Cooker Carnitas

Servings: 8

Ingredients

2 bay leaves

¾ cup of chicken broth

1-2 chipotle peppers (diced)

2 tablespoons of adobo sauce

1 teaspoon of cumin

½ teaspoon of pepper

1 teaspoon of oregano

¾ teaspoon salt

3-4 minced garlic cloves

1 diced onion

2 ½ pounds of pork shoulder, lean

Directions

Season your pork with salt and pepper then place in a Crockpot. Combine the rest of the ingredients in a bowl and pour over the pork. Cook on low for at least 6 hours until your pork shreds easily. Pre-heat your oven to 500F and lay your pork out in one layer on a non-stick baking sheet then roast for 5 minutes or until the edges are toasted and crispy.

Nutritional information per serving

224.9 calories, 28.5 g of proteins, 1 g of fiber, 1.3 g of carbohydrates, 7,7 g of fat

Slow Cooker Pork Tenderloin

Servings: 6

Ingredients

2 lb pork tenderloin

3 tablespoons soy sauce

Black pepper to taste

¾ cup red wine

1 cup water

1 (1-ounce) envelop dry onion soup mix

3 tablespoons minced garlic

Directions

Put the pork tenderloin in a crock pot as well as the soup mix contents. Add wine, soy sauce and water ensuring to coat the pork. Spread garlic over the pork carefully then sprinkle some black pepper. Cover and cook on low for four hours.

Nutritional Information per serving

Calories: 337.7, Protein: 45.1g, Total Carbs: 2.4g, Dietary fiber: 0.2g, Sodium: 638.9mg, Cholesterol: 119.4mg

Slow Cooker Creamy Pork

Servings: 4

Ingredients

16 ounces lean pork tenderloin, cut into half-inch cubes

2 cloves garlic, minced

2 yellow onions, sliced

2 tablespoons sweet paprika

2 tablespoons parsley, chopped

½ cup low fat Greek yogurt

1/8 teaspoon cayenne pepper

1 bay leaf

1 ½ cups chicken stock

Directions

Place a skillet coated with non-stick cooking spray over medium heat. Add the pork and cook for around 3 minutes or until no longer pink.

Transfer this pork to a crockpot and return the pan to heat, coat with more non-stick cooking spray and add garlic and onions. Sauté these for three minute ensuring that you stir occasionally. Add in cayenne, paprika and ¼ cup of stock into the pan and stir vigorously then pour this into the crockpot with the rest of the stock and bay leaf.

Cook for five to seven hours on low until the pork is tender. Turn off heat, remove bay leaf and stir in the parsley and yogurt. Serve immediately.

Nutritional Information per serving

Calories: 211.2, Protein: 34.4g, Total Carbs: 7.7g, Dietary Fiber: 2.2g, Cholesterol: 82.6mg, Sodium: 77.8mg

Slow Cooker Pulled Pork

Servings: 12

Ingredients

2.5lb pork roast

1 can diced green chiles

1 can tomatoes with diced green chiles

2 teaspoons taco seasoning

½ cup chopped onion

3 cloves of garlic, minced

1 teaspoon cayenne pepper

Directions

Pour the can of tomatoes with green chiles into the slow cooker and place the pork on top. Mix the can of green chiles and other ingredients and slather on the surface of the roast. Cook on low for around 8 hours then shred the pork and return to the cooker and mix this with the juices. Heat for a few minutes until heated through then serve.

You can eat this with some whole grain bread or better some vegetables.

Nutritional Information per serving

Calories: 250.2, Total Fat: 18.2gProtein: 18.1g, Total Carbs: 2.3g, Dietary Fiber: 0.4g, Sodium: 157.9mg, Cholesterol: 71.0mg

Slow Cooker Pork Chops

Servings: 13

Ingredients

2.5lbs boneless pork cutlets

¼ cup olive oil

1 tablespoon poultry seasoning

4 garlic cloves, minced

½ cup chopped onion

1 teaspoon dried basil

1 teaspoon dried oregano

1 tablespoon garlic powder

1 tablespoon paprika

½ teaspoon black pepper

1 cup chicken broth

½ tablespoon salt

Directions

Cut some small slits in the pork and place in the slow cooker. Whisk the other ingredients then pour over the pork. Cook for four hours on high or for 6-8 hours on low heat ensuring to baste periodically.

Nutritional Information per serving

Calories: 230.1, Protein: 24.8g, Total Carbs: 2.0g, Dietary Fiber: 0.5g, Sodium: 348.6mg, Cholesterol: 61.9mg

Slow cooker Cream of Mushroom Pork Chops

Servings: 4

Ingredients

4 boneless pork chops

1 cup water

1 can cream of chicken soup

1 can cream of mushroom soup

Directions

Brown the pork chops in frying pan then add the cream of mushroom soup in the slow cooker. Add the pork chops to the slow cooker then the cream of chicken soup. Cook for 5-6 hours on high or 7-8 hours on low.

Serve this with brown rice or vegetables.

Nutritional Information per serving

Calories: 284.6, Protein: 23.2g, Total carbs: 10.6g, Dietary Fiber: 0.0g, Sodium: 1022.0mg, Cholesterol: 57.2mg

Slow Cooker Pork Loin Roast

Servings: 8

Ingredients

1 ½ lb boneless pork roast

¼ cup olive oil

4 garlic cloves, minced

1 chopped onion

1 tablespoon paprika

1 tablespoon poultry seasoning

1 teaspoon basil

1 can fat free chicken stock

1 teaspoon oregano

1 tablespoon garlic powder

½ teaspoon black pepper

½ tablespoon salt

Directions

Mix all the ingredients except the pork roast and rub this over the roast. Place the roast in slow cooker and add chicken stock. Cook for 8-10 hours on low or 4-6 hours on high.

Nutritional Information per serving

Calories: 197.4, Protein: 18.9g, Total Carbs, 4.1g, Dietary Fiber: 1.1g, Sodium: 897.0mg, Cholesterol: 44.7mg

Low Carb Slow Cooker Beef Recipes
Low Carb Crockpot Mexican Pot Roast

Servings: 8-10

Ingredients

1 teaspoon of garlic powder

1 beef bouillon cube

1 (12 ounce) bottle of Frank's hot sauce

2 tablespoons of chili powder

8 ounces of canned green chiles

½ cup of yellow onion, sliced

1 teaspoon of olive oil

1 teaspoon of pepper

1 teaspoon of salt

3-4 pounds of boneless beef chuck roast

Directions

Mix all the ingredients in a slow cooker. You can opt to cut the roast in half if you are using a smaller crockpot. Cook it on high for approximately 6 hours or until the roast is fork tender. Serve with favorite low-carb sides of your choice like broccoli.

Nutritional information

Approximately 18g net carbohydrates

Coffee- Braised Brisket

Servings: 8 (1/4 cup of cooked onion and 3 ½ ounces of cooked meat)

Ingredients

1 tablespoon of balsamic vinegar

½ cup of strong brewed coffee

2 large sliced onions

1 (3-pound) boneless beef brisket

1 teaspoon of salt

1 teaspoon of ground black pepper

1 teaspoon of garlic powder

1 tablespoon of paprika

1 tablespoon of ground coffee

2 tablespoons stevia

Directions

Mix stevia, paprika, garlic powder, pepper, salt and ground coffee. Trim any fat from the meat and rub the mixture over the brisket. If need be, you can cut the meat. Put the meat in a slow cooker and place the onions over the brisket then mix vinegar and coffee, and pour over onions. Cover then cook on low-heat setting for 10 hours or on high heat setting for 4 ½ hours. Transfer the meat to a cutting board and slice the meat across the grain. Remove the onions with slotted spoon from the cooking liquid. Serve it with meat.

Nutritional information

229 calories, 32g of proteins, 5 g of sugars, 1 g of fiber, 8 g of carbohydrates, 417 mg of sodium, 98 mg of cholesterol, 8 g of fat.

Crockpot Low Carb Phillycheese Stick

Servings: 4 (1 ¼ cups) servings

Ingredients

1 tablespoon Zesty Italian dressing

8 ounces of sliced fresh mushrooms

32 ounces of sliced fresh mushroom

1 (32 ounce) box of beef broth

¾ cup of thinly diced yellow onion

1 green pepper, diced

1 ½ pounds of thinly sliced beef round steak

1 tablespoon butter

Directions

Except the butter, dressing and cheese, add all the other ingredients to your slow cooker and cover. Cook on low for about 8 hours or high for about 4 hours or until it is tender and thoroughly cooked through.

Drain the meat and veggies then slice the meat and sauté it together with the veggies in a little butter together with the Italian dressing on high until they are lightly browned all through. Top this over lettuce.

Nutritional information

5g of net carbohydrates per serving

Low Carb Crockpot Cabbage Rolls

Servings: 12 cabbage rolls

Ingredients

1 cup of no sugar added marinara sauce

½ teaspoon of pepper

A handful of fresh chopped parsley

1 teaspoon of onion powder

2 minced garlic cloves

1 cup of parmesan cheese

1 pound of ground beef

12 large cabbage leaves

Directions

Cook the cabbage leaves in hot water for 3 minutes to soften them slightly. Place ½ cup of the marinara sauce into the crock pot and mix the ground beef, minced garlic, parmesan, parsley and pepper together in a medium bowl. After the cabbage leaves have cooled down enough, measure about ¼ cup of the meat filling into the bottom of each cabbage leaf. Bring sides of the leaf together over meat filling and then roll the leaf up. In case the leaves are a bit narrow, put them side by side overlapping slightly to make a cabbage roll. Put the cabbage rolls into the slow cooker with the seam side facing down. Top rolls with the rest of ½ cup marinara sauce and cook on high for approximately 5 hours.

Nutritional information

Approximately 2g of net carbohydrates per cabbage roll

Slow cooker Taco Beef

Servings: 12

Ingredients

3lb ground beef

1 teaspoon salt

1 cup water

2 teaspoons cumin

2 teaspoons chili powder

½ teaspoon Oregano

1 teaspoon onion powder

1 teaspoon garlic powder

Instructions

Put the beef at the base of the crockpot and break it up using a spoon. Add some water and cook for five hours on low. Drain water and fat from meat and stir in spices then return to the heat for another hour.

Nutritional Information per serving

Calories: 303, Protein: 20g, Fat: 24g, Carb: .5g

Beef chuck pot roast

Servings: 10

Ingredients

1 onion soup dry mix (use 1 packet)

1 can celery soup

4 lbs beef roast

Directions

Use a fork knife, stab the meat in different places and transfer it to the slow cooker with side with most fat facing up then add dry onion soup on top and on the sides. Add the can of celery soup over the roast and then spread a little on top. Cover and cook on high for 3 hours and on low for 5 hours.

Nutritional information

Calories: 280, Carbohydrates 2.5 g, sodium: 397.4 g, cholesterol: 117.9 mg, Total fat: 13.2 g, Protein: 35.5g, Dietary Fiber:0g

Eggplant Bolognese

Servings: 8

Ingredients

1 lb lean ground beef

4-6 garlic cloves, minced

1 diced onion

1 ½ lbs eggplant, chopped

¾ teaspoon salt

1-2 bay leaves

½ cup Parmesan cheese

1 (28-ounce) can whole tomatoes

½ cup chicken broth

½ teaspoon pepper

Heat a non-stick pan over medium high heat then add garlic, the meat, onion, pepper and salt then cook for around 10 minutes until browned.

Transfer the browned meat to the crock pot and add the rest of the ingredients then cook on low for 6-8 hours or until the eggplant breaks down completely.

Nutritional Information per serving

Calories: 146.9, Protein: 15.9g, Carbs: 8g, Fat: 6.1g, Fiber: 2.6g

Low Carb Slow Cooker Turkey Recipes
Slow Cooker Collard Greens

Servings: 12 (½ cup servings)

Ingredients

2 tablespoons of olive oil

3 tablespoons of apple cider vinegar

½ cup of water

1 teaspoon of salt

2 teaspoons stevia

1 (14.5 ounce) can fat free chicken broth

½ large chopped onion

2 pounds of chopped collard greens

6 ounces turkey meat (such as turkey necks)

Seasoning to taste (black pepper, chili powder, garlic powder,)

Directions

Put the turkey meat at the base of a slow cooker. Add onions and the collards. Add the water and chicken broth. Cover with a lid and set a timer on high for 6 hours. When the collards have cooked for about 45 minutes, add in the stevia, the salt, the olive oil and the rest of the ingredients then stir. Cook until the collards have reached the desired texture.

Nutritional information per serving

49.6 calories, 3.4 g of proteins, 0.5 g of dietary fiber, 2.3g of carbohydrates, 366.8mg of sodium, 11.3 g of cholesterol, 3.1 of fat

Split Pea Soup

Servings: 8

Ingredients

7 cups of water

4 chicken bouillon cubes

10 ounce turkey ham, cubed

3 whole bay leaves (or 1 teaspoon or crumbled)

1 medium white onion (coarsely chopped)

1 cup baby carrots, coarsely chopped

16 ounce package split peas

Directions

Rinse peas before you cook them.

Add all the ingredients to a crockpot and cook during the day when at work or overnight on low.

Nutritional information per serving

Calories: 122.7, Protein: 11.8g, Dietary fiber: 5.2 g, total carbohydrates: 15.0 g, Sodium: 780.6 mg, cholesterol: 24.0 mg, fat: 2.0g

Low Carb Crockpot Turkey Soup

Servings: 8-10

Ingredients

½ tablespoon extra virgin olive oil

1 cup diced celery

½ cup chopped onion

2 (10.75 ounce) cans chicken broth

2 cups chopped, turkey

2 cups chopped turkey breast

1 cup fresh spinach

2 cups shredded cabbage

6 spear asparagus

1 cup of sliced mushrooms

4 cups turkey broth

Directions

Sauté onion and celery in ½ tablespoon olive oil in a skillet. Add all broth and water to slow cooker. Add in all the chopped veggies including sautéed onion and celery, turkey and dried Italian seasoning as well as salt and pepper. Cook for 4-6 hours on low or until veggies are soft.

Nutritional Information per serving

Calories: 123.3, Protein: 16.6g, Total Carbs: 5.3g, Fat: 4.1g, Dietary Fiber: 1.3g, Sodium: 1086.7mg, Cholesterol: 41.9mg

Crock Pot Turkey Breast

Servings: 14

Ingredients

6-7 lbs bone-in turkey breast

1 teaspoon minced garlic

1 tablespoon olive oil

1 teaspoon seasoned salt

1 teaspoon Italian seasoning

1 teaspoon paprika

½ cup water

1 teaspoon pepper

Directions

Brush the turkey with olive oil then mix the seasoned salt, garlic, Italian seasoning and paprika and rub this on the turkey. Place the turkey in a slower cooker, add water, cover and cook for 5-6 hours on low.

Nutritional Information per serving

Calories: 174, Protein: 37g, Fat: 2g, Sodium: 172mg, Cholesterol: 101mg, Trace Fiber and Carbohydrate

Crockpot Sesame Turkey

Servings: 8

Ingredients

3 lbs turkey breast tenderloins

1/8 teaspoon cayenne pepper

¼ teaspoon black pepper

¼ cup reduced-sodium soy sauce

1 tablespoon lemon juice

¼ cup reduced-sodium chicken broth

4 teaspoons grated ginger

2 cloves garlic, minced

1 tablespoon toasted sesame oil

2 tablespoons cold water

2 tablespoons cornstarch

1 tablespoon toasted sesame seeds

2 tablespoons green onion, sliced

Directions

Place the turkey in a slow cooker and sprinkle with cayenne pepper and black pepper. Combine chicken broth, ginger, soy sauce, lemon juice, garlic and sesame oil then pour this over the turkey in the slow cooker. Cover and cook for 5-6 hours on low or 2 ½ -3 hours on high.

Nutritional Information per serving

Calories: 222, Protein: 42g, Fat: 3g, Carbs: 3g, Cholesterol: 112mg

Slow-Cooked Turkey Legs with Mushrooms

Servings: 4

Ingredients

1 tablespoon tomato paste

1 onion, halved and sliced

1 (8-ounce) package button mushrooms, quartered

1 cup low-sodium chicken broth

2 lbs turkey legs

2 teaspoons dried parsley

2 cloves garlic, minced

Salt and pepper

½ teaspoon dried tarragon

½ teaspoon marjoram

Directions

Season the turkey legs with pepper and salt. Brown the turkey legs in a pan over medium heat. Once browned, remove from pan and put aside. Add half of the stock to the pan and scrap the browned bits. Add tomato paste into the broth and loosen it up.

Add onions, mushrooms and garlic to a slow cooker, layer the turkey legs on top and add the broth-tomato mixture and the remaining broth then sprinkle with the herbs.

Cook on high for 6-8 hours or on low for 8-10 hours. Serve the meat and pour over the tomato sauce and vegetables.

Nutritional Information per serving

Calories: 330.7, Protein: 54.1g, Fat: 9.6g, Carbs: 4.3g, Saturated Fat: 3.1g, Sugar 0.8g, Sodium: 475.3mg, Cholesterol: 229.0mg

Lemon-Herbed Turkey Breast

Servings: 4

Ingredients

2 lbs turkey breast

1 teaspoon rosemary

¼ cup lemon juice

2 tablespoons Dijon mustard

1 teaspoon oregano

2 cloves garlic

Salt and pepper to taste

½ cup dry white wine

Directions

Put all the ingredients (with the turkey skin side down) in the slow cooker and cook for 6-8 hours on low making sure to baste the turkey if need be.

Nutritional Information per serving

Calories: 355, Protein: 45g, Fat: 15g, Carbs: 3g

Savory Turkey Breast

Servings: 12

Ingredients

6 ½ lb bone-in turkey breast

1 chopped stalk celery

1 chopped onion

½ cup water

½ teaspoon freshly ground black pepper

½ teaspoon salt

1 bay leaf

1 teaspoon chicken bouillon granules

Directions

Place celery, bay leaf and onion in cavity of turkey. Place turkey in the slow cooker, sprinkle with pepper and salt.

Mix bouillon with water until dissolved then pour over the turkey. Cover and cook for 8-9 hours on low. Remove the bay leaf, serve turkey and enjoy.

Nutritional Information per serving

Calories: 352, Protein: 49g, Fat: 16g Carbs: 1g

Low Carb Slow Cooker Vegetable Recipes
Crockpot Cream Of Zucchini Soup

Servings: 4 cups of soup

Ingredients

1 tablespoon regular whipping cream

¼ teaspoon pepper

1 tablespoon butter

½ cup of chopped yellow onion

4 cups chopped with peel green zucchini squash

2 cups of beef or chicken broth

Directions

Mix all the ingredients in your crock pot just leaving out the whipping cream then cook for about 5 hours on low or until zucchini is tender-soft. Puree the soup in a blender. Stir in the whipping cream then serve.

Nutritional information per serving

79 calories for every cup of soup, approximately, 4.3 g carbohydrates

Flavorful Matzo Balls

Servings: 8

Ingredients

Broth

¾ teaspoon of ground turmeric

1 teaspoon of pepper

1 teaspoon of salt

2 tablespoons of snipped fresh dill

¼ cup of minced fresh parsley

1 medium leek, sliced (white part only)

2 medium onions cut into wedges

3 small turnips, peeled and cut into chunks

3 medium carrots (cut into chunks)

2 parsnips, peeled and cut into chunks

12 garlic cloves (peeled)

10 cups of water

Matzo balls

8 cups of water

¾ cup whole grain matzo meal

1 ½ teaspoons of salt (divided)

3 tablespoons of rendered chicken fat

3 tablespoons of water

3 eggs (separated)

Directions

For the broth:

Mix all the broth ingredients in a crockpot and bring to a boil. Lower the heat and cover then simmer for 2 hours. In the meantime, beat egg yolks in a large bowl on high speed for about 2 minutes. Add ½ teaspoon of salt, water, and the chicken fat then in another bowl, beat the egg whites on high speed until stiff peaks emerge. Fold this into yolk mixture then fold in your matzo meal cover and place in the refrigerator for about 1 hour.

Bring water and the remaining salt to a boil in another stockpot, then add eight rounded tablespoons of matzo dough in boiling water. Cover and lower the heat then simmer for 25 minutes. Do not lift cover when simmering.

Remove the matzo balls using a slotted spoon. Put in a bowl and pour some soup over the matzo ball.

Nutritional information per serving

100 calories, 3 g protein, fiber traces, 7 g carbohydrate, 322 mg sodium, 83 mg cholesterol, 7 g fat (2 g saturated fat)

Slow Cooker Minestrone Vegetable Soup

Servings: 10

Ingredients

1 medium yellow onion, chopped

¼ cup fresh parsley, chopped

3 cloves garlic, chopped

1 cup broccoli, chopped

2 cups celery, chopped

5 cups water

3 beef bouillon cubes

2 cups cauliflower, cubes

2 cups zucchini, quartered and chopped

¾ cup grated parmesan cheese

Salt and pepper to taste

2 cups green beans, chopped

A small handful of fresh basil, finely chopped

Directions

Add all ingredients to slow cooker. Cook for 8 hours on low until vegetables are tender. When vegetables are tender, remove 2 cups of the vegetables and puree in a food processor or blender then return the pureed vegetables to the soup. Once warmed through, allow the soup to cool before adding the parmesan cheese.

Nutritional Information per serving

Approximately 4.15g net carbs

Low Carb Crock Pot Vegetable Soup

Servings: 6

Ingredients

8 ounces fresh mushrooms, sliced

2 (14-ounce) cans beef broth

1 (14-ounce) can diced tomatoes

1 green pepper, chopped

1 yellow onion, chopped

1 zucchini sliced thinly

4 ounces turkey, sliced

Mozzarella cheese for topping

1 teaspoon stevia

1 ½ tablespoons basil leaves

½ teaspoon salt

Directions

Put the broth, veggies, tomatoes, stevia, salt and basil in a slow cooker and mix thoroughly. Top with the turkey slices then cook on low for 8 hours or high for 4 hours. Pour into bowls and top with the cheese.

Nutritional Information per serving

Calories: 125.2, Protein: 11.9g, Carbs: 11.6g, Total Fat: 3.9g, Saturated Fat: 0.7g, Dietary Fiber: 2.7g, Sodium: 1720.9mg, Cholesterol: 24.5mg

Crockpot Vegetable soup

Servings: 10

Ingredients

5 ¼ cups vegetable broth

4 cups water

3 carrots, peeled and chopped coarsely

1 head of cabbage, cored and chopped coarsely

½ lb zucchini, chopped coarsely

½ lb chopped white mushrooms

½ lb peeled and chopped onion

4 garlic cloves, minced

½ teaspoon crushed Herbs de provence

¼ teaspoon salt

¼ teaspoon pepper

½ teaspoon thyme

¼ lbs cut into thirds green beans

Directions

Mix all the ingredients in the crockpot except the carrots. Set crock pot to low heat then cook for four hours.

Transfer ½ of vegetables to a blender and puree with ½ cup broth then put aside. Transfer the other half of the remaining vegetables to the blender and puree until coarsely chopped.

Return the chopped and pureed vegetables to the crockpot, stir to mix then divide among serving bowls and garnish with some carrot.

Nutritional Information per serving:

Calories: 79, Fiber: 5g, Protein: 4g, Fat:1g

Slow Cooker Spinach Souffle

Servings: 6

Ingredients

20 ounces spinach, chopped

½ cup mayonnaise

8 ounces cream cheese

¼ cup grated onion

¼ teaspoon white pepper

2 eggs, beaten

½ cup cheddar cheese, shredded

Directions

Mix spinach with onion and beat remaining ingredients then add in spinach mixture. Spoon the mixture into a slow cooker that has been greased and cook for 2-3 hours on high heat.

Nutritional Information per serving

Calories: 351, Fat: 34g, Protein: 10g, Carbs: 6g

Crock Pot Zucchini Parmigiana

Servings: 4

Ingredients

3 thinly sliced zucchini

1 cup tomato sauce

½ cup ricotta cheese

3 tablespoons parmesan cheese, grated

1 teaspoon Italian seasoning

½ cup Mozzarella cheese, grated

Directions

Combine the Italian seasoning and tomato sauce then put this mixture into the crock pot. Mix the mozzarella and ricotta cheese then place a layer of zucchini followed by the cheese mixture in the crock pot and repeat this process. Pour the remaining sauce over the top and sprinkle with parmesan. Cook for 2-3 hours on low.

Nutritional Information

Calories: 155, Protein: 11g, Carbs: 10g, Fat: 9g

Spinach Casserole

Servings: 6

Ingredients

20 ounces frozen spinach; thawed, drained and chopped

3 eggs

1 tablespoon almond flour

¼ cup butter

2 cups cream style cottage cheese

1 ½ cups cheddar cheese

1 teaspoon salt

Directions

Combine the cheddar cheese, butter and cottage cheese and add the spinach to the cheese. Beat the eggs slightly and add to the spinach mixture and stir. Add the flour and salt to the spinach mixture.

Grease a crock pot and put the spinach mixture then cook for 4-5 hours on low or 1 hour on high.

Nutritional Information per serving

Calories: 325, Protein: 22g, Fat: 22g, Carbs: 10g

Conclusion

I want to thank you so much for your purchase and your time. I hope that you can now add some variety to your daily meals with these slow cooker recipes I have provided you. I know you and your family will just love them all!

The only real question left is which one will become your favorite?

If you finding it hard to eat well at work or school then I am going to recommend you check out a free preview on the next page of "Mason Jar Meals - Amazingly Delicious And Easy To Make Recipes For Meals On The Go." Now you can eat better and save money while on the road or at work or school. I think you will really enjoy it.

Thank-you

Sara Banks

Free Preview Mason Jar Meals

Jalapeno, Creamed Corn And Cheddar Cornbread

Servings: 3

Ingredients

1 cup of shredded sharp cheddar cheese

2 medium jalapenos (diced finely)

1/3 cup of grated onion

1 cup of creamed corn

2 eggs

1 cup of buttermilk

½ teaspoon baking soda

2 teaspoons of baking powder

1 teaspoon of salt

2 cups of yellow cornmeal

Directions

Whisk the cornmeal, the salt, the baking powder, and the baking soda in a medium bowl. In another larger bowl, whisk the butter milk, the eggs, the onion, the creamed corn and jalapeno. When well combined, add dry ingredients to wet mixture and stir vigorously. Lastly, fold in the cheese.

Fill a wide mouth mason jar with a cup of leftover chili then scoop 1/3 of cup plus one heaping tablespoon of cornbread batter over the chili. Bake for around 25 minutes or until a toothpick inserted at the center comes out clean. It is best to let the jars to cool completely before covering them with the lids.

Thai Peanut Tofu Spread

Yield: 5 cups

Ingredients

1/3 cup of chopped peanuts or cashews

1 bunch of scallions (thinly sliced)

½ cup of chopped cilantro

¾ cup of finely diced bell pepper

1 cup of shredded carrot

3 tablespoons of sugar

2 tablespoons of rice vinegar

1/3 cup of tamari

1 teaspoon chili paste

½ cup of coconut milk

½ cup of peanut butter

2 peeled cloves of garlic

1 ½ inch piece of ginger (quartered and peeled)

20 ounces of extra firm tofu (high protein)

Directions

Squeeze the extra liquid out of the tofu. Use two cutting boards to slice the tofu longitudinally into two thin pieces and wrap them in a clean kitchen towel that will help in absorbing the excess liquid. You need to do this so as to make sure the tofu will absorb the recipe liquid instead. Pulse the garlic and the ginger in a food processor until minced finely. Open the processer from time to time and scrap down the sides and process again until you are satisfied it is all well processed. Add the chili paste, the peanut butter, the coconut milk, sugar, rice vinegar and tamari. Pulse in the food processor until well blended, this will take around one minute.

Split the tofu into several small pieces then add them to the peanut mixture. Process in the food processor until the mixture is well blended and the tofu should be chopped into smaller pieces by this time. Place the remaining mixture in a medium bowl and fold them in the rest of the ingredients.

You can pack a mason jar with around ½ a cup of the tofu spread in ½ jar pint Mason jar together with a mason jar of cucumbers and carrots then add another half-pint with whole wheat flat bread.

Preserved lemon pasta

Servings: 8

Ingredients

4 ounces of pecorino (shredded)

¾ cup of flat leave parsley (chopped)

1 (15-ounce) can of chickpeas

½ cup of halved Mo....

Made in the USA
San Bernardino, CA
06 January 2016